FATHER TO THE
FATHERLESS

4th Book

With

Sam & Sasha

Speak it Kiddo Publishing LLC.

Greenville, Sc.

Edited by: Alex Mills

Published by Speak it Kiddo Publishing LLC.
All Rights Reserved

ISBN-13: 978-1727022872
ISBN-10: 1727022874

It was Father's Day at school,
and everyone's father was there.
Everyone's except mine,
thought Sam and Sasha.
There were so many times when they said,

I wish my father were here.

At my basketball game,
I looked into the crowd,
and my father wasn't there.
**I wish my father
were here.**

Johnnie's father was teaching him
how to play baseball.

I wish my father
were here.

I wish my father were here
to read me a bedtime story.

I wish my father were here.

I had a tea party today
with my Barbie dolls.
**I wish my father
were here.**

I got all A's on my report card!
I wish my father were here.

I would love to have
my father here fishing with me.
I wish my father
were here

I want my father to teach me
how to ride my new bike.
I wish my father
were here.

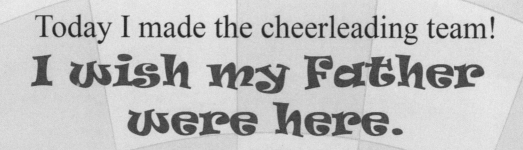

Today I made the cheerleading team!
I wish my Father were here.

I would love for my father
to teach me how to tie my tie.
**I wish my father
were here.**

My mommy had a big birthday party
for me today!
**I wish my father
were here.**

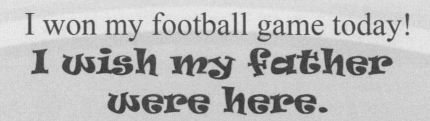

I won my football game today!
I wish my father were here.

Today was my first dance recital.
I wish my father were here.

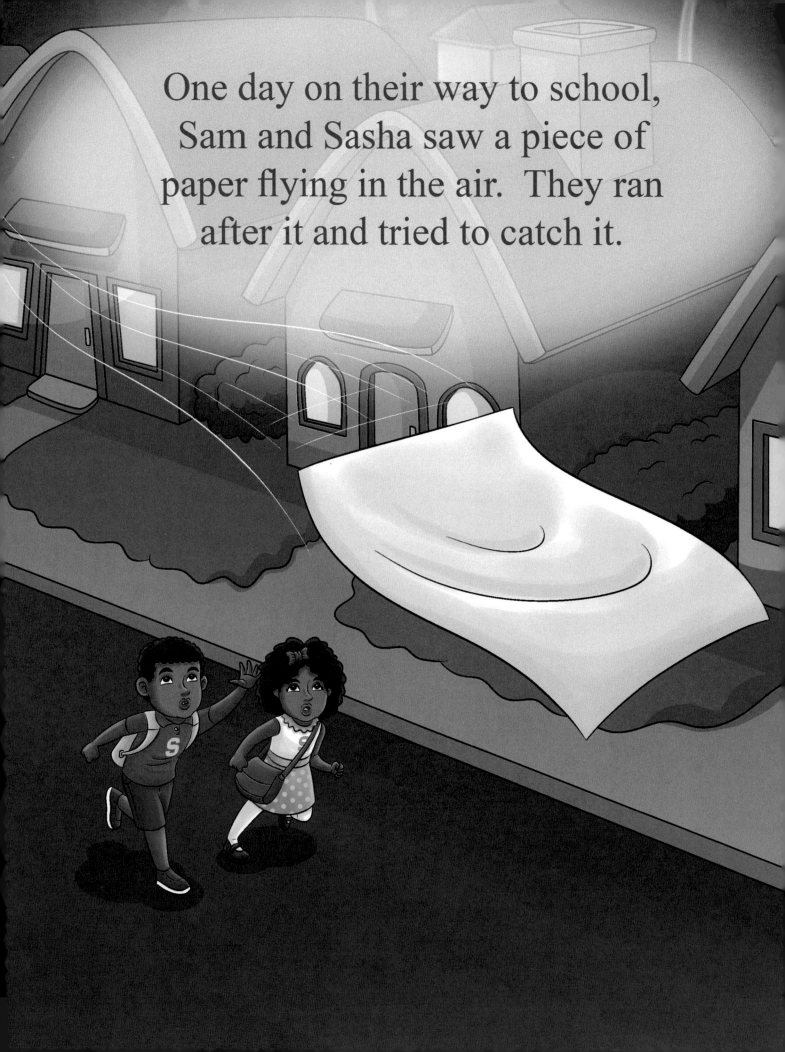

One day on their way to school,
Sam and Sasha saw a piece of
paper flying in the air. They ran
after it and tried to catch it.

They ran, they jumped, but couldn't seem to catch the piece of paper.

Finally, they were very tired and decided to stop and sit down on a bench.

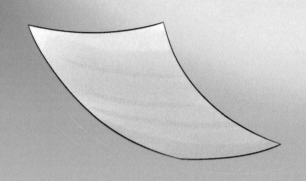

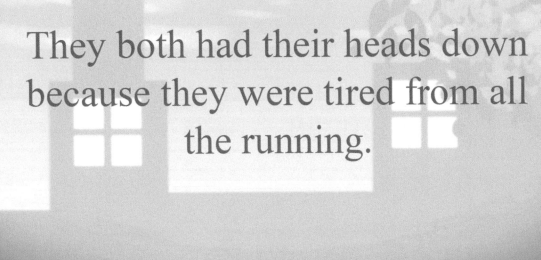

They both had their heads down
because they were tired from all
the running.

Suddenly, the piece of paper landed in a puddle of water on the ground right next to them.

With wonder and excitement,
they picked up the paper!

Together they read the piece of paper.

They tried to read the rest but couldn't see it clearly because the paper was wet.

Psalm 68:5
I am a Father
to the Fatherless

Hurriedly they ran to Mr. Jean's house. They asked Mr. Jean, "What does this mean?" Then they read the piece of paper to him "I am a Father to the Fatherless."

Mr. Jean said, "You both have a heavenly Father who is always watching over you. He goes with you everywhere you go. The heavenly promise is that he is a Father to the Fatherless. He promises that he will never leave you."

Sasha thought for a moment, and then said, "Was he at my recital?" Mr. Jean replied, "Yes, he was there."

Sam asked, "Was he at my football game?" Mr. Jean said, "Yes Sam, he was there."

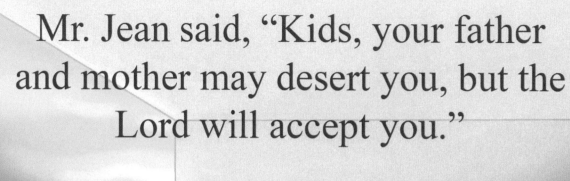

Mr. Jean said, "Kids, your father and mother may desert you, but the Lord will accept you."

They told Mr. Jean goodbye. Mr. Jean smiled and said, "Goodbye kids."

It made Sam and Sasha happy to know they had the heavenly promise that God is a Father to the Fatherless.

And, because they have a heavenly Father who is always with them, they don't have to feel alone anymore!

Sam and Sasha were very happy, and they begin to say out loud; "I have a heavenly Father who loves me. He watches over me. He never leaves me. He calls me fearfully and wonderfully made. And I will become all that my heavenly Father has called me to be, because my heavenly Father is a Father to the Fatherless."

JAMES EDWARD WILLIAMS

is the bestselling author of several children's

In light of his most recent book, Father to the Fatherless, James grew up without the presence of a loving father to offer him guidance through life's growing pains, to cheer him on from the gym bleachers at games, or to pull him into a warm embrace at the sight of him in his cap and gown. Despite his tragic childhood though, his unwavering faith and determination has moved him to look towards God to fill that shadowy void of a fatherly figure.

He has since made a career out of reaching out to today's fatherless youths – whether it be that their fathers are not fully present in the relationship, or physically absent from their lives. Finding God's calling in Houston, Texas, he has written books in hopes to influence children to defy the odds in pursuit of their dreams, to build a future that's bigger than themselves while remembering their Heavenly Father, the God of All Comfort, who will by no means leave them, nor forsake them.

Follow the Author
jamesedwardwilliams.com
@jamesedward.williams
@speakitkiddo
Facebook / James E. Williams

Made in the USA
Columbia, SC
05 April 2022

58537232R00020